BRAZIL

LETTERS FROM AROUND THE WORLD

Patrick Cunningham

Photographs by Sue Cunningham

CHERRYTREE BOOKS

LETTERS FROM AROUND THE WORLD

Titles in this series

BANGLADESH · BRAZIL · CHINA · FRANCE · INDIA · ITALY · JAMAICA · JAPAN · KENYA · SPAIN

A Cherrytree Book

Conceived and produced by

Nutshell
MEDIA

Intergen House
65-67 Western Road
Hove BN3 2JQ, UK
www.nutshellmedialtd.co.uk

First published in 2003 by
Evans Brothers Ltd
2A Portman Mansions
Chiltern Street
London W1U 6NR

VISIT OUR WEBSITE
www.evansbooks.co.uk
Evans

Editor: Polly Goodman
Designer: Tim Mayer
Map artwork: Encompass Graphics Ltd
All other artwork: Tim Mayer
Geography consultant: Jeff Stanfield, Geography
   Inspector for Ofsted
Literacy consultant: Anne Spiring

All photographs were taken by Sue Cunningham.

Printed in Hong Kong.

Acknowledgements
The photographer would like to thank the Soriano family,
the Fernandes family and the staff and pupils of Rio de
Janeiro School for their help with this book.

British Library Cataloguing in Publication Data
Cunningham, Patrick
   Brazil. – (Letters from around the world)
   1. Brazil – Social conditions – 1985 – Juvenile
   literature
   2. Brazil – Social life and customs – 20th century –
   Juvenile literature
   I. Title
   981'.064

ISBN 1 84234 185 5

Cover: Julio (centre) with his friends Daniel and Salvatore
   on Copacabana Beach.
Title page: Julio (left) with his friends João and Lucas
   swinging in a hammock.
This page: A flooded part of the Amazon Rainforest.
Contents page: Julio practises a handstand.
Glossary page: Parrots in Rio's Botanical Gardens.
Further Information page: Iguaçu Falls.
Index: A view over the city of Rio de Janeiro.

Contents

My Country

Saturday, 3 May

Avenida Borges 6412
Apartment 347
Rio de Janeiro, RJ
CEP 23129-000
Brazil

Dear Jo,

Bom Dia! (You say 'Bom jee-ah'. This means 'good day' or 'hello' in Portuguese, Brazil's main language.)

My name's Julio Soriano and I'm 8 years old. I live in Rio de Janeiro, a big city in Brazil. We call it Rio for short. I have one little sister, Sofia, who is 4.

I can help you with your class projects on Brazil.

Write back soon!

From

Julio

This is me with Sofia, Mum and Dad, outside our flat.

Brazil is so big that both the Equator and the Tropic of Capricorn run across it.

Brazil's place in the world.

Brazil is the biggest country in South America and the fifth-largest country in the world. It has borders with ten other countries.

Rio de Janeiro means 'River of January' because in January 1502, Portuguese explorers thought they had discovered the mouth of a river. But Rio is on a big bay, not a river mouth.

High-rise office and apartment blocks are squeezed between Rio's hills.

Rio used to be the capital of Brazil. In the late 1950s, a new capital city called Brasília was built in the middle of the country. Rio is still an important business centre and a busy port.

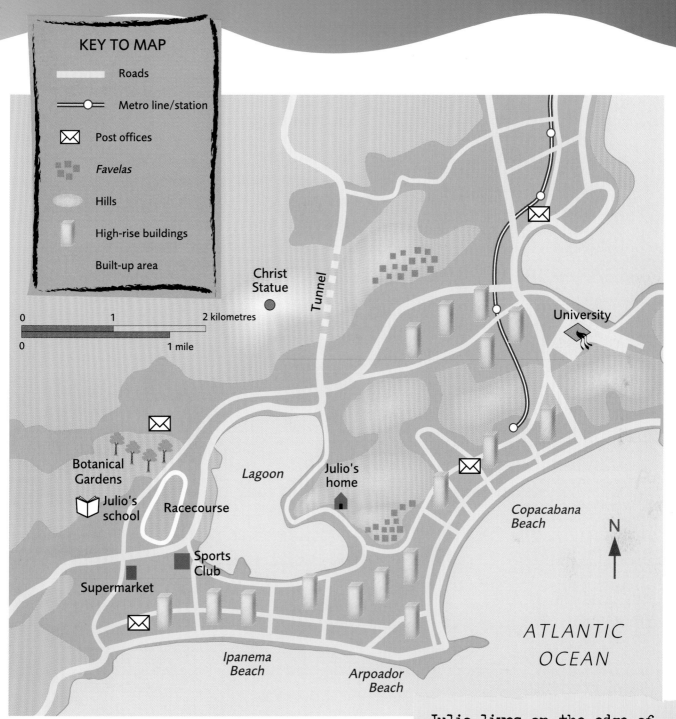

KEY TO MAP

▬▬▬	Roads
▬◯▬	Metro line/station
✉	Post offices
▦	*Favelas*
⬭	Hills
▯	High-rise buildings
	Built-up area

0   1   2 kilometres
0   1 mile

Christ Statue

Tunnel

University

Botanical Gardens

Julio's school

Racecourse

Lagoon

Julio's home

Copacabana Beach

Sports Club

Supermarket

ATLANTIC OCEAN

N

Ipanema Beach

Arpoador Beach

Julio lives on the edge of a lagoon. It is close to two of Rio's biggest beaches, Copacabana and Ipanema.

Most of Rio is built on flat land, but there are several steep hills. Poor people build their homes on the hillsides, in areas called *favelas* (you say 'fa-vell-ah'). The streets of Rio are often jammed with traffic. It can be quicker to use the metro to get around.

Landscape and Weather

Rio is one of many natural harbours on Brazil's long coastline. Outside the city there are coffee and sugar-cane plantations. In the north of Brazil is the vast Amazon Rainforest.

Rio is in the tropics, so it is hot all year round. In tropical storms it can rain very hard. Houses in Rio's *favelas* sometimes get washed away in the floods.

Large areas of the Amazon Rainforest are flooded for part of each year.

Rio is lined with
long sandy beaches
and rocky shores.

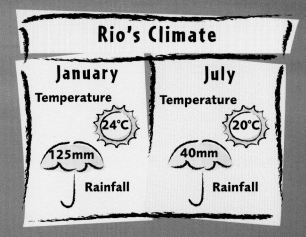

Rio's Climate

January	July
Temperature	Temperature
24°C	20°C
125mm	40mm
Rainfall	Rainfall

ESCOLINHA Fla
ESCOLA OFICIAL
DO FLAMENGO

BARRACA da DILMA

At Home

Like most people in Rio, Julio's family lives in a flat. It is on the fourth floor of a tall apartment block, beside a lagoon. There are three other flats on the same floor. The block has eleven floors altogether.

This is the view from Julio's flat. You can see across the lagoon and the high-rise buildings to the sea the other side.

When Julio's grandmother comes to visit, the family often sits out on the balcony.

Julio's flat has two bedrooms, a living room, a kitchen and two bathrooms. There is also a small study. Outside there is a balcony, with a high fence to stop anyone falling over the railing.

The living room has a television, video, stereo and Julio's computer games.

Sofia and Julio have bunk beds. Julio sleeps in the top one.

Julio and Sofia share a bedroom. They can see right across the lagoon from their bedroom window. If he goes to bed after Sofia is asleep, Julio has to be really quiet.

Julio's dad has a computer in the study. Sometimes he lets Julio play games on it.

Monday, 5 July

Avenida Borges 6412
Apartment 347
Rio de Janeiro, RJ
CEP 23129-000
Brazil

Oba! (You say 'or-ba'. This means 'hi' in Portuguese.)

It was great to get your letter yesterday. Have I told you about the play area we've got at home? It's on the ground floor of our apartment block. There are swings and a slide, which Sofia likes, but I prefer the table football. The floor's really smooth for practising skateboard tricks, too.

Write again soon!

From
Julio

Here I am playing table football with Dad.

Food and Mealtimes

Julio's family usually has lunch together. Maria the maid helps prepare the food.

For breakfast, Julio has cereal and a milk shake. Lunch can be chicken and salad or fresh vegetables. Black beans and rice is a favourite Brazilian dish.

In the evening, Julio's family sometimes has fish with *mandioca frita* – fried cassava chips. There is always lots of fresh fruit.

Julio's mum does most of the shopping in the local supermarket. Sometimes she buys fruit and vegetables from market stalls, which are set up every Saturday near the flat.

In the supermarket, people use the *real* (you say ray-al) to buy food. The *real* is the currency in Brazil.

Julio buys a coconut with its top cut off so he can drink the juice through a straw.

Thursday, 20 August

Avenida Borges 6412
Apartment 347
Rio de Janeiro, RJ
CEP 23129-000
Brazil

Hi Jo,

Thanks for the recipe you sent me. Here's one for you. It's for Brazilian sweets, called *brigadeiros* (you say 'brig-a-dare-us'):

You will need: 1 tin sweetened condensed milk,
4 heaped dessertspoons cocoa powder, 25g butter,
grated chocolate

1. Put the condensed milk in a saucepan with the butter.
2. Stir over a medium heat until the butter has melted.

3. Add the cocoa powder
   and stir until it goes gooey.
4. Remove from the heat
   and let the mixture cool.

← This is my gran
helping me stir the
chocolate mixture.

Everyone likes rolling the chocolate balls. It's very tempting to lick your fingers!

5. Take a teaspoonful of the mixture and roll it into a ball.
6. Roll the ball in the grated chocolate and put it on a plate.
7. Do the same until all the mixture has been used.

Write and tell me what you think of them.

From
Julio

Lots of *brigadeiros*, ready to be eaten – yummy!

School Day

In Brazil, some children go to school in the morning and some go in the afternoon. Julio goes to school from 1 p.m. until 5.15 p.m. His dad usually drives him there after lunch, on his way back to work.

Children who live nearby walk to school. Others travel by car or by minibus.

At Julio's school, girls and boys wear the same school uniform — a white t-shirt and blue shorts.

Julio's class learns English, maths, science, history, geography, music and art. They also learn Portuguese, which is Brazil's main language.

Julio and his friends Lucas and Pedro draw pictures in an art class.

The long school holiday is in the Brazilian summer, from mid-December to the end of January. There is also a winter break of three or four weeks in July.

Friday, 15 September

Avenida Borges 6412
Apartment 347
Rio de Janeiro, RJ
CEP 23129-000
Brazil

Bom Dia Jo!

I'm glad you liked the *brigadeiros*. At school this week we did a special project about teeth. They're called *dentes* (you say 'den-chis') in Portuguese. We made a poster with a diagram of a tooth and the names of all the different teeth. We included photos of food that is good for your teeth, like fruit and vegetables. I'm going to try not to eat too many sweets because they rot your teeth. Then you have to go to the dentist and have a filling.

Write soon!

From
Julio

This is the poster we made for our teeth project.

Off to Work

Julio's dad is a lecturer at Rio's university. He teaches his students about tourism. When they finish university, some of the students will work in hotels and travel agencies. Some will become tour guides, helping holidaymakers who visit Rio.

Julio's dad teaches his students in a classroom at the university.

This trader is selling towels to tourists on Copacabana Beach.

Lots of people work in offices in Rio. The city is an important business centre. Other people in Rio work in shops or factories.

Outside Rio, this man is squeezing the juice out of sugar-cane. It will be sold as a drink.

Outside the city, there are lots of jobs on plantations growing oranges, coffee and sugar-cane. Orange juice from Brazil is exported all around the world.

Free Time

Julio and his friend Lucas see who can do a handstand for the longest. Julio's record is 9 seconds.

Everyone in Rio loves the beach. Whenever he can, Julio goes there to surf, or just to play on the sand.

Sometimes Julio goes to the sports club just across the lagoon from his flat. He can play tennis and swim in the pool there.

Volleyball is a popular game on Rio's beaches.

Julio's family often visits the Botanical Gardens. There are lots of flowers, trees, monkeys and colourful parrots to see.

Colourful parrots and other birds fly about high in the trees of the Botanical Gardens.

Religion and Festivals

The Christ Statue is on the highest hill in Rio. It overlooks the whole city.

Most Brazilians are Roman Catholics, but there are other religions, too. Many people whose ancestors were African still follow African religions.

Everyone takes part in the Carnival celebrations in February. The whole country has a holiday. The last day of Carnival is Shrove Tuesday.

These girls are dressed in their special Carnival costumes.

Sunday, 14 February

Avenida Borges 6412
Apartment 347
Rio de Janeiro, RJ
CEP 23129-000
Brazil

Hi Jo,

It's been really exciting here because it's Carnival time! Last Friday we went to watch the big procession through the streets. Everyone dressed up. I wore the Carnival costume that Mum helped me to make. The noise of the drumming was deafening. I had to stick my fingers in my ears! Everyone on the street was dancing samba. The next day we went to a Carnival party. There were lots of musicians playing samba tunes.

Do you celebrate any special festivals?

From
Julio

These costumes were amazing!

Fact File

Size: 8,547,404km^2

Population: 170.1 million. Brazil has the fifth-largest population in the world.

Flag: The green and yellow colours stand for forests and minerals. Inside the yellow diamond is a blue sphere, with a star for each of the 26 states and Brasilia's Federal District. Across the sphere is written the motto *Ordem e progresso*, which means 'order and progress'.

Capital city: Brasília is the capital of Brazil. It was built in the 1950s in the middle of the country. Before Brasília, Rio was the capital, and before Rio the capital was Salvador.

Other major cities: São Paulo is Brazil's biggest city. Rio de Janeiro is the second-biggest city. Other major cities are Belo Horizonte, Salvador, Fortaleza, Curitiba, Recife, Porto Alegre, Belém and Manaus.

Neighbouring countries: French Guiana, Surinam, Guyana, Venezuela, Colombia, Peru, Bolivia, Paraguay, Argentina and Uruguay.

Languages: Portuguese is the main language. There are also about 120 native Amerindian languages. Immigrant groups speak their own languages as well as Portuguese. Some of these are Japanese, Italian and German.

Highest mountain: Pico da Neblina (3,014m).

Currency: The *real* (R$). There are 100 centavos to one *real*.

Longest river: The Amazon is 6,577km long. It is the second-longest river in the world. Ocean-going ships can navigate all of the Amazon in Brazil.

Biggest waterfall: The Iguaçu Falls are one of the natural wonders of the world. They lie along the border between Brazil and Argentina.

Main industries: Iron, steel and aluminium, motor vehicles, electronic goods, coffee, sugar, orange juice and soya beans.

Famous Brazilians: Alberto Santos Dumont was one of the first people to make and fly an aeroplane, in 1906. Many people say that Pelé was the greatest football player ever.

Main religions: Most Brazilians are Roman Catholic, but there are also Muslims, Jews and Shinto followers. In the north-east, many people still follow African religions, such as Candomblé and Umbanda.

Stamps: Brazilian stamps often show Brazil's wildlife, or musical instruments that are used to play Brazilian music.

Glossary

Amerindian The name given to the people who were already living in South America before explorers arrived from Spain and Portugal.

ancestors People who lived before you, from whom you are directly descended. Your grandparents are your ancestors.

Bom Dia (you say 'Bom jee-ah') The greeting used by Brazilians in the morning. It means 'Good day'.

Carnival The most important Brazilian festival, 40 days before Easter. Processions of decorated lorries tour the streets. People dress up in fancy dress and there is lots of music.

cassava A root vegetable, like potatoes.

Equator An imaginary line that runs around the middle of the Earth.

exported Sold abroad.

favela An area of cheap housing built by poor people.

lagoon A lake connected to the sea or a bigger area of water.

metro An underground railway.

plantations Large farms where only one crop is grown.

procession A large number of people moving together.

river mouth The part of a river where it meets the sea.

samba A Brazilian dance with an off-beat rhythm that started in Africa.

sugar-cane Tall grass which contains sugar in its sap.

tourism The business of providing services to holidaymakers.

Tropics The regions either side of the Equator, between the Tropics of Cancer and Capricorn.

Further Information

Information books:

B is for Brazil by Maria de Fatima Campos (Frances Lincoln, 1999)

The Changing Face of Brazil by Edward Parker (Hodder Wayland, 2001)

Continents: South America by Mary Virginia Fox (Heinemann, 2001)

Country Insights: Brazil by Marion Morrison (Hodder Wayland, 1999)

Fiesta!: Brazil by C. Phillips (Franklin Watts, 2001)

A Flavour of Brazil by Mariana Serra (Hodder Wayland, 1999)

A Visit to Brazil by Peter Roop (Heinemann, 1998)

We Come from Brazil by Andre Lichtenberg (Hodder Wayland, 1999)

Fiction:

How Night Came from the Sea: A Story from Brazil by Mary-Joan Gerson (Little, Brown & Co, 1994)

The Sea Serpent's Daughter: A Brazilian Legend by Argentina Palacios (Troll Books, 1993)

Websites:

CIA Factbook
www.cia.gov/cia/publications/factbook/
Basic facts and figures about Brazil and other countries.

Viva Brazil.com
www.vivabrazil.com
A virtual trip to Brazil.

Index